Community, Culture, and Me

Written by
Gavin Worthy

Helping in the Community

KidHaven
PUBLISHING

Published in 2027 by
KidHaven Publishing, an Imprint of Greenhaven Publishing, LLC
2544 Clinton St., Buffalo, NY 14224

Written by: Gavin Worthy
Edited by: Doug Barone
Designed by: Ker Ker Lee

Cataloging-in-Publication Data

Names: Worthy, Gavin.
Title: Helping in the community / Gavin Worthy.
Description: Buffalo, NY : KidHaven Publishing, 2027. | Series: Community, culture, and me | Includes glossary and index.
Identifiers: ISBN 9781534570047 (pbk.) | ISBN 9781534570054 (library bound) | ISBN 9781534570061 (ebook)
Subjects: LCSH: Community life--Juvenile literature. | Community organization--Juvenile literature. | Helping behavior--Juvenile literature.
Classification: LCC HT65.W678 2027 | DDC 307--dc23

Printed in China

CPSIA compliance information: Batch #QS27KH: For further information contact Greenhaven Publishing LLC at 1-844-317-7404.

Please visit our website, www.greenhavenpublishing.com.
For a free color catalog of all our high-quality books,
call toll free 1-844-317-7404
or fax 1-844-317-7405.

Find us on

Photo Credits – Images courtesy of Shutterstock.com, unless otherwise stated.

Cover & Recurring – Rawpixel.com, PeopleImages.com, Dedraw Studio, TVhappyLine, Africa Studio, Gorodenkoff, Bradericon. 2–3 – Pixel-Shot. 4–5 – PeopleImages, New Africa. 6–7 – JU.STOCKER, Sorapop Udomsri. 8–9 – David JC, andysavchenko. 10–11 – Eric Johnson Photography, SpeedKingz. 12–13 – TommyStockProject, Molenira. 14–15 – Dave Smith 1965, Monkey Business Images. 16–17 – CandyRetriever, PeopleImages. 18–19 – ggcarrle, jakamn. 20–21 – UrbanArtr, Pixel-Shot. 22–23 – six o'clock, Jhon Percy Ticona Mamani.

Contents

Words that look like **this** can be found in the glossary on page 24.

All Together Now

A community is a group of people who have something in common. A community could be made up of people from the same school or people who like the same sport.

What communities are you part of?

It's good to share and help each other in a community. Sharing and helping others is great for everyone. For example, it's much easier to do all the chores at home when everyone helps.

Volunteering

Volunteering is when you choose to spend your time helping people, animals, or the planet. You don't get paid for volunteering. People volunteer because they want to help.

Volunteering is a great way to help in your community.

You could help your town or city community by volunteering in a park and picking up litter. Some people volunteer by giving out food to people who need it.

You could volunteer by visiting a nursing home.

Looking After Animals

Animals can be a big part of communities. There are lots of ways to help them. You could plant seeds to grow wildflowers—these are great for bees! Make sure to use native seeds.

You could plant your seeds in a community garden.

You can also volunteer at or raise money for an animal shelter in your town or city. This is a place that helps animals that do not have a home.

Being Nice to Neighbors

A neighbor is a person who lives in the home next to you or in the same area as you. You can spread kindness in your community by helping your neighbors.

Smiling and being friendly toward others spreads kindness.

Talk to a parent or guardian about ways you can help your neighbors. Your family could help an elderly neighbor by shopping for them. You could also help with their household chores.

Even just sitting down to talk with neighbors can help them.

Donating

You can help your community by donating things. You could give food to a food bank. Food banks give out food to people who are struggling to afford it.

Donating means giving.

You can also donate money to a charity. A charity is an organization that does helpful things. Charities can help people, animals, and more!

Charities need help and donations to continue working.

Raising Money

Communities need money to run projects and improve things. You can raise money for a community in lots of ways. You could hold a raffle and give the money you make to a local charity.

Always ask an adult to help you when you want to raise money for something in your community.

You could be sponsored for something. This is when people agree to give you money for a charity if you do something. Many people do sponsored runs, walks, or reading challenges.

You could have a bake sale to raise money for a good cause.

Community Spaces

Many communities have spaces where people can meet. These might be libraries, community centers, schools or parks. It is important to look after these community spaces.

You could help by cleaning up a community space.

Just going to a community space can be helpful. The more people who use a community space, the stronger the community becomes. What community spaces could you visit more often?

Books

Have you ever seen a Little Free Library? These are small boxes on the street with books in them. The idea is that a book is free to take, but you should leave another book in its place.

Little Free Libraries are great ways to share books with your community. Ask an adult to help you set one up. You could be in charge of making sure it has enough books.

Protecting the Planet

The global community includes everyone. Everyone lives on the same planet, which makes it the biggest community of all. It's everyone's job to look after our global community by protecting the planet.

There are lots of ways to protect the planet.

You can help protect our global community by looking after the environment. If you can, walk or bike to places instead of going in a car. You could even take public transportation, such as the bus.

Recycling glass, plastic, and paper stops them from going into a landfill.

It Starts with You

Could you help a community? You could have a bake sale at your school or volunteer at an animal shelter. Or could you join a new community?

Schools and libraries are good places to build new communities.

You might like to create your own community. All you need to do is find people who have something in common with you. What community would you make?

Whatever you decide, one thing is true—it starts with you.

Glossary

environment the natural world

landfill where waste is buried

local describing an area close by

native originally coming from or growing in a certain area

organization a group of people that work together for a particular purpose

Index